I'll See You Thursday

I'll See You Thursday

POEMS BY

Myra Shapiro

BLUE SOFA PRESS

Edited by Robert Bly
ISBN #0-9638722-2-2

Grateful acknowledgment is made to the editors of the following publica-
tions in which these poems appeared as they are or in slightly different
versions: *Ailanthus*, "On Dug Gap Road," "Topless Dancer in a Dressing
Room"; *Café Solo*, "The Disappearance"; *Calyx Journal* (forthcoming Winter
96/97), "The Inheritance"; *Kalliope*, "Over and Over," "This Heart"; *Footwork:
Patterson Literary Review*, "Holiday Mornings"; *Pearl*, "Marriage: February,
1953," "How I Learned to Kiss"; *Ploughshares*, "The Woman Who Said Excuse
Me"; *The Poetry Miscellany*, "A Miniature at the Metropolitan," "Shrikes";
River Styx, "Towers: Century City, LA"; *Southern Indiana Review*, "Paint,"
"The Cadences of Southern Kindness"; *Staple 29* (Derbyshire, England),
"How I Learned to Kiss."

"The Corset" was collected in *Bubbe Meisehs by Shayneh Maidelehs*, ed.
Lesléa Newman (Santa Cruz: HerBooks), 1989.
"The Disappearance" also appeared in *Jewish Women's Literary Annual*
prepared by The Jewish Women's Resource Center, NY, NY, 1994.
"Each Night" was collected in *Women's and Men's Liberation: Testimonies
of Spirit*, ed. Leonard Grob, et al. (Westport, CT: Greenwood Press), 1991.
"Hating Unhappiness" is forthcoming in *Marilyn My Marilyn*, Pennywhistle
Press.
"Passover" was collected in *Education for Peace; Testimonies from World
Religions*, ed. Haim Gordon, et al. (Maryknoll, NY: Orbis Books), 1987.

The italicized line in the last verse of "Towers: Century City, LA" is from
"The Plot Against the Giant" by Wallace Stevens, *The Collected Poems of
Wallace Stevens* (New York, NY: Knopf), 1971.

I'll See You Thursday is the third volume in a series from Blue Sofa Press: a
cooperative effort, operated and funded by artists and writers. Blue Sofa
was created to make available some of the work that has grown out of the
Great Mother and New Father Conference, now in its twenty-second year.

BLUE SOFA PRESS
Distributed by Ally Press
524 Orleans Street, Saint Paul, Minnesota 55107
1-800-729-3002
http://www.catalog.com/ally/

Author's Acknowledgments

I wish to thank Dorset Colony House and The MacDowell
Colony for the support and solitude provided by fellowships,
Vermont College for its writers and program, and the Great
Mother community for its great women and new men.

And my thanks to the poets—friends and teachers—in this
city where I live: in particular, Lee Briccetti, Priscilla
Ellsworth, Victoria Hallerman, Wendy Larsen, Sabra Loomis,
Mary Jane Nealon and Susan Sindall, to Fran Castan, Barbara
Elovic, Ingrid Hughes and Marnie Mueller, Bob Holman,
Colette Inez, Galway Kinnell and Sharon Olds. Thanks to Fran
Walzer and Fran Quinn, to Haim and Rivca Gordon, and
Rosalind Solomon, to Robert Spalding, Gloria Friedman,
Margaret Kornfeld, Renée Gorin and Jack Wiener. Thanks to
D.M. Stein for his energy and Benjamin for his metaphors.

To Robert Bly I give my heartfelt thanks for his generosity, for
his vision and courage to make community, for questions in
tiny script that went to the center of my heart.

To Sophie
      who always knows what side she's on

For my husband, Harold
For my daughters, Karen and Judith

"If I live and be well I'll see you tomorrow; if not
I'll see you Thursday."
Ida Stein

Contents

One

Two

One

A Miniature at the Metropolitan

Two lovers wind around each other
curved like countries on a globe.

The father and the mother I'd come on
those mornings in each other's

arms, her braids undone, sprawled
on his freckled skin,

her gown turned inside out, silken
underside of vines

after their so fierce quarreling
all evening long. Such secrets pull

me to this man from Isfahan—
                                    his hand moves

toward her breast, her cinnamon
robe splits for his arm—

languorous Persian pleasure—and I'm allowed
to see—a man and woman

loving, in a wilderness
of boughs made for endless ardor.

Holiday Mornings

1. *Sister*

My father had to dislodge the star
from my sister's throat. I had put it there.
Asked to care for her when she was one
I didn't know of sex then—
my parents closed their door—
only of happiness at being made the mother
for an hour, and for a toy
I gave her something silvery,
my charm, a Jewish star. How could I know
she'd swallow it? Still today I can't say how
my father, naked, performed
the miracle, held her crooked
until she coughed into his palm the star.

2. *Dime*

He handed me a dime, though we were poor,
to buy a paper and—*take your time* —
any candy I desired. I knew
I'd choose a Frozen Twist, iced marshmallow
inside the dark, curled chocolate.
Across a Coney Island lot
to the store four blocks away I ran
and let it drop. The coin
lay buried somewhere in that sand. Afraid
to go back home, ashamed
for so much lost, I walked into a mystery:
my mother's laugh, my father's lifting me.

Marriage: February, 1953

The night before our wedding day I took
A fit. My mother, who said she hadn't cried
Like that when her first baby died, shook
Me—too many fittings? showers?—to take pride
In my fine man, in what I'd planned: angora
Sweater, dinners by candlelight, perfume
On my arms, White Shoulders, its aroma
Would take us to an island place, a room
Unknown, our very own. Pioneers. Married
I cooked, he waited to be fed. His work
Did not go well, we moved. Pumpkin-headed
I wandered aisles, staring. Pick up. Put back.
Spring. On Hibiscus Court hibiscus bloomed.
I longed to be back home, getting married.

The Song She Always Sang

She is my mother or the song
my mother sang. Pinned round

dark braids make a crown.
In a tunic stitched with red

embroidery, a dirndl skirt,
the girl is entering

the meadow. Air hollows
for her shape, her figure opening

the grass. She will fill her hands
with daisies, and a soldier

on a hike nearby will spy
black braids, her blouse

caught up with wind. He'll promise
if she loves him

he'll return. She hears
her mother's warning, but her heart

is now the meadow. She takes him
in. Each Spring,

withdrawing to the rock,
she listens to the wind. I listen

to a life spent longing—
my mother's, the song's—

and I become her look-out—
where is he? when will he

come to me?

On Dug Gap Road

for my sister Raina

We see him laughing with his chest exposed.
He's moved us to a wilderness
from an apartment near a park, to a house
with red clay hills and a yard of evergreens
where he stands declaring he will buy
a shotgun, he and gold-toothed Peewee
are going out to hunt. But just
*look at the moon, Ida, come out
and give a look!*
          She walked right off the landing,
the unprotected porch, straight down
to the ground. That first night—

So much for the moon. Crude, showy
braggart, she called the energy
that always took her breath away,
his rushing out next day
to line the porch with flowers,
boxes he'll paint green, four chairs
he'll hammer, and *look
at the flowers, Ida,
dahlias and sweet william—*
          wanting her, wanting
attention. And Mama, she hid her dreams
not to fall with his.

How I Learned to Kiss

A movie actress taught me. She crept inside
a bed to warm a man who had a chill;
he was an outlaw but she had to
save his life, her body had to do that.
Her hair, her breasts, her vivid
darkened mouth opening towards him
made me ache for Saturday when I would
wet my lips, move forward
in the back seat toward the stranger
pressing close, breathing hard, insistent on
the power of a star.

Family Jokes

"He hath made me to laugh, so that all who hear
will laugh with me." Sarah, GENESIS 21:6

They always liked a good joke. Even a bad one.
The one about the eighty year old man
who takes a young wife. "A fatal marriage,"
his neighbor warns. "Fatal, shmatal,"
he replies, "if she dies, I'll take another."

Jokes are what they had, my folks
who scared me so with troubles
and loud arguments. In the middle of
my mother's unfulfilled desires,
my father's failures, working day and night

to make a living—you call this living?!—
came the joke. The breather. The sun
to warm us. The moon was sex,
a mystery you needed to deflect
by making light: a young man

asks a young girl if she'd like to
take a walk in Prospect Park, and then
he's getting fresh with her. She protests,
"What do you think I am, a prostitute?!"
He says, "Who's talking about money?"

They laughed. Immigrants, they bundled
loss. I don't know when my mother coupled
sorrow with sweet impudence to coin
her favorite exit line: "If I live and be well I'll see you
tomorrow; if not, I'll see you Thursday."

Stucco in Paradise

Before I am nine
we live without four walls
with relatives who take us in
sometimes in the middle of the night—
my father trying to make a living
travels, my mother lost
is beautiful, songs
fill her heart with dreams
entering America, singing
"When You Wore a Tulip"
with my father who wears spats
and takes her out of the dark tenement,
the bathroom down the hall, carries her off
to Erie, Pennsylvania. But where is
her family? He holds her
with a baby, Shirley like Shirley Temple,
and then the good one dies. Lost
my mother wants to leave him,
take her beauty, begin again.
She is trying to leave him.

They are hugging on the sofa
that makes into a bed
in Tante Annie's living room.
She will be pregnant with me.
We live I don't know where . . . all the arguments
who can hear or get a word in.
There are bedbugs in the middle of the night
so we are knocking on the door of Tante Annie
where we are always welcome
with her children and their children

trying to make the world a better place
especially for the working class.
Pictures of Mexican peasants, music,
books fill every nook. Friends in every room.
Food always on the table.

On the road my father is selling curtains
and in a booth called Linens and Domestics
he sits at the World's Fair.
My cousin takes me there, takes me
to the Russian Pavilion, a whole day,
our lunch packed in a paper suitcase.
Early one morning I wake, my Tante near,
where is my mother? my mother
(who for the first time that very winter
stood with me and my father: the three of us!
in line for *Snow White and the Seven Dwarfs*)
is gone and Tante says I have a baby sister

so people come to see, bringing chocolates in a tin
my mother fills for the rest of her life
with threads and needles. My sister like my mother
sings "God Bless America," and soon
my father moves us
to the bedspread center of the world
where it is calm but far away.
He comes home every night, and we eat
around a table, but in the bedroom late at night
they are still arguing, though not as much
as when we had no house. And in this place
Dalton, Georgia, I have to think how to talk
and how to play with Virginia Woodson
and Margaret Looper. They hear my story
of the Jewish star but then
they don't know what a Jewish star is.

The Cadences of Southern Kindness

When I tried on the woolen sweater
coarse ribbed wool
and the salesclerk gushed
How Sweeet!
my stomach pitched
back to the April of my greenhorn days—
kinky-haired outsider, brassy kid
brought from the Bronx
to a rosiness as puzzling as thorns.
Caught at hide and seek I spit
You sonuvabitch!
to who was It, and every kid
shrank from me, stopping play.

I had to whip my words
with air. They said
say ma'am to get *sweet* milk
at lunch, *may I ma'am?*
to use a *rest* room. But *Huh?!*
was all I knew.
Sweet milk turned out to be a carton
of plain pasteurized
and later when I ran to rest
the room was dark green rows
of sinks and toilets
the Spring my father's powerful hope moved us
South to make a buck.

On Being Pushed When I Was Seven

He threw me in the bay
and I refused to rise.
A friend convinced him
children swim by nature.
So would I. His child,
daughter of the show-off
fighter, I held myself
down, damned
if I'd perform
for any father's friend
who never even glanced
at me. And down there
I took the time
to swear and plan and look
at bubbles coming
from my mouth.
Those men who pulled me
out, they had to pump
like mad. They were the ones
who had to dance.

The Corset

The corset of my Tante Annie
held her to the symmetry
of her youth—an immigrant
sent south to help her uncle
tend his store (I want to shelter her—
the broken English, the strangeness
of a Jew, of a body at fourteen).
She was alone. Four boys ganged her.
For one year she had to stay in an asylum.

No one told. North, she met her husband
whose artistic, fluent ways enabled her
to ripple like a fountain. But not so fast—

first she grew fat, so that each morning,
bone by bone, a corset laced the chaos
to its parts: full breasts, slim waist,
round hips: a figure eight to match my age
those summer nights I shared her room
and saw the miracle, how, stay by stay,
lace by lace, she loosened the reined flesh
and sent it tumbling—*ahh a machaiah!* —
fold by fold, sigh by sigh, the drench of it
so delicious I told everyone
when I was grown I wanted fat
like hers, vast and operatic.

Paint

To be a lousy god
hurts. You create
children, writings, a deck
off the side of the house—
here's your chance to build from scratch—
and your work fails. You face the paint
that's uglier than knotty wood
you chose to cover, the child
you refuse to support, the word
you lose in one frill
after another: effort
bent on grace. Beauty, kindness
always *almost* there . . .
remember sweet, red cedar,
remember your daughter's hand
the bud of it in yours
as you crossed the boulevard, remember
beef and bones, soup
boiled to a consommé.
The smell of a dream is all
you can catch this morning
when the bell rings, wakes you
to the door, to the roofer
holding an estimate for the roof
shot full of holes from hail.

To Jerusalem, 1990

It's a *sheroot*, that's what
Israelis call a jitney, a car for hire,
layering nine people—more—in tiers,
our baggage rope-tied overhead
like the upper layer in a dig,
the jumble of us a somehow-

linked-together carload underneath.
Three Hassidim (black coats, black hats)
insist on sitting separate;
they climb in back. No smile, no greeting,
they want no part of me, a woman
without a wig or scarf to hide my hair.

One cradles a little girl on his lap
whispering to her from time to time,
not in Hebrew but in Yiddish:
Mameleh, du vilst shpillen?—
language of my childhood, labials that cling
like steamed milk to its cup.

So when the man who coos the child
tells the others where he lives is good—
you don't see any gentiles, you don't see
any dirt—*me zet nit kayn goy,
me zet nit kayn shmutz*—I burn.
He means my son-in-law

is filth, my daughter's love
is unacceptable. In sounds that sing
he spits. This is the homeland, we
are related, but home, he says, is his.
There it is—Jerusalem—suddenly
on its hill—and I am not prepared.

Two

Stuck in Ordinary Life

To be desperate is a terrible thing.
To be prisoner or unable to breathe
pushes your face against the pane
as if to break it, as if
plunging through would draw you up
instead of down. Out of Gaza we cross
the checkpoint and barbed wire and
speed away in our shiny rental—
but yesterday visiting family, my cousin
and his wife bickering, bickering,
I would kill myself, I said,
before I'd end in a marriage
like theirs. Why kill, there's always
divorce, my husband tried to tell me
but I felt extreme as a prisoner, shut up
in the hatred of a father and mother, no breath
to build a bridge and I wanted to jump.

My Husband Sits

I wanted out. I wanted streets
but most of all I wanted
a dusk of unfamiliar people

where every life seemed possible.
As from a book. To be anonymous.
Men I didn't know took shape

every class I took: on the white tile
of a lab, down the aisle
of a mezzanine. Off the curb

at Michigan or Vine, lights
going *come on, come on,*
Go, my hair began to sway

from its barrette. But I didn't fall,
I climbed. At the teacher's feet
I took on Emma Bovary, a mother

I had to know. Pound and Eliot
played hard to get, rebuffed me
so I felt dirtied, sometimes

desperate, but tough. I went places
through those books, and reached a center
that stayed put, even through a war.

Each Night

What Scott Fitzgerald called the green breast
of the new world I see when I look at you

each night you pull into our driveway
home from work, home to me,

holding in your look the sweetest dream
that's possible. Your face does that—

each night your smile is fresh, an innocence
that says this place is God's

and she is inside waiting to receive me.
The pleasure of that expectation

on the roundness of your face never fails
to step into the light; each night it promises

I will be loved for being here and being me.
Our hug holds that belief. Yet

in five minutes—how are we betrayed?
Your face goes flat, my voice grates shrill; you

need TV and tire early. I stay up
to find my way with someone in a book.

Hating Unhappiness

I know the perfect woman
for my husband to marry.
In a big glass house, high
on a hill, land rolling out below,
he could be simply him, the center
of attention, and everywhere
he'd go everyone would say
How ya doin' which is all
the friendship he'd need,
having the center of affection
at his side, blonde hair
curled right, jet beads from him
on her satin blouse, traveling
with him to Istanbul, cruises,
islands of the South Pacific. For him
I wish I could be her. Marilyn.
As Chinese women in *The Good Earth*
arrange concubines for their men,
I hand him to her. To get him off
my mind, release the struggle of
my heart to see him happy.

The Wind

Weird though it may be, there's nothing sexier than summer
wind sailing through

a screen so that I put my book aside to let it love me.
Today it came, an unexpected

riffling through the branches of a hickory tree, unexpected
since nothing moves

in Tennessee in mid-July; dead heat
lifts only for a storm

flashing—a moment—leaving not this breeze
but air that's lead, not this

gaiety spilling seeds through the magnolia leaves.
Of course I dropped my book—

such luxury in motion, mingling heat
and gentleness teased me

to make love to myself, which is delicious—

but then Paolo and Francesca
flew into my head, lovers Dante visits early

in a hell that's hardly hell and yet
it is, hot wind they'll forever circle in, hearts bound

by what they read, to longing, to a kiss,
to you, dear Dante, coming here yourself to hand

me warning, to lift my nose
out of a book and walk me past the porch, the open window.

The Woman Who Said Excuse Me

She suddenly disappears. Flows
into a crowd, into a subway
from which she'll refuse to emerge.
The reporter will write: "She plunged
into the crowd at the annual summer festival
and never returned. The children
found their way to their father alone."

She does not die. She does not desire
the father, mother, even the sister
who wait with all that insistence.
Remember how the mother
of Odysseus in the underworld
flung her sadness in his face.
To disappear requires a wilderness.

"She had a husband and children
and two months of events
written into her calendar." Years
of making love, rounds
of kindnesses. The circle
will not do. It takes
some angled thing to cut through
conversations. As when you say *Excuse me,*
I am going to use the bathroom. Go.

Paint your face with seeds from inside
a thistle plant, walk west
all afternoon with smeared red
on your forehead, cheeks, the tip

of your nose. "An unidentified driver
dropped her off at the intersection
of routes 12 and 115. That's where the trail ends."

On the beach of a river.
In the white room of a cell.
In the Arctic. Where others disappear
she is not lost. For years she sat with maps.
To go forth, nothing is better.

The Fit

He'd left me,
not saying that he'd left me,
not gone, but
                    the fit
that comes from every absence
that is present, from the person
who unclicks you in his head,
                              who says
he's in your life but isn't
there, like a curb within a dream
you put your foot down from and suddenly
                                        no landing
you're falling, the step is air.
All the business of the dresser
I shoved off: papers, paper clips,
                              my museum
calendar, tickets to *Les Miz,* tickets
for a flight to Chattanooga
cluttered the carpet to the bed: the thousand proofs
                                                  we live
getting somewhere, always
planning, arriving—then the vanishing
as if the other is too much to bear.
                              Dirty clothes
stuffed in the hamper
I pulled out, and this time sorted
not to do a wash but just to
                              erect mountains:

slips, bras, pantihose,
socks, undershorts, and shirts. Evidence—
that's not it but what is felt by it when

                                          it couples

with a word like *hard*—hard
evidence I needed underneath my feet.
I had to step on piles of it to sleep.

Shrikes

Cast-iron skillet, cut-glass
Cornucopia, hobnailed vase,
Copper pitcher, neck narrow
And pointed. These
Went fast when we
Sold my mother's
Belongings.
And when one woman
Picked up the worn pyrex,
Wanting to bargain for a quarter
Wanting a cover thrown in as well,
I snapped
Two quarters, you gimme
Two quarters
And let the coins warm my palm.

Over and Over

The smell of soup, the warm room
say bone to me, say marrow. Curled
on a cushion in the breakfast nook
I'd read from *Adventures in Reading*
to Mama. Over and over
I chose "Thanatopsis." I was moony
over death, the grave
a couch for lying down to dream.
All that breathe
will share thy destiny.
She listened, washing dishes
in front of the window. Mimosa
dropped its feathery blooms,
pink mess on the patio.

Go forth under the sky, I rhapsodized,
longing for a fate with kings, the wise,
the good—oh earth that would
so generously make a bed for us.
And Mama ended up in Florida
in a high-rise by the Bay,
"Moon Over Miami" rising with her
in the elevator. Released
from kitchen chores she played
the dogs at night. And when
she died—it wasn't right—
she didn't want one friend
to see. I will not go like that.
I want a bridge—maybe poems,
maybe trees, northern, wild, free.

Passover

This year a sister-in-law is dying.
An English-Hebrew fills our mouths
around a table
set with wine, soup, for each
a chopped piece of fish,
the ritual of this family for years.
She stands to bless us—
all other years her husband
has been the one to rise—
she prays—*Oh shit*—
to regain speech from tears.

We sing *Dayenoo*; my husband's palm
taps mine to make his father's rhythm
stay alive. Plagues have fallen
diminishing our cups, ten drops
of wine. And we sing sorrow,
we sing satisfied, grateful
for protection, for the soul
set free. Linked
to this house by my will,
how will *I* separate to speak a rage
rising? On my milk-white plate
a coral cobra's running wild.

* * *

Die Ay Noooo . . . all night
I hear in broken sleep
the kitchen clock stop
start stop start, the spigot
driveling in the basin. It's five years
since my mother died—
the stammer
of this quiet house is pain
I want to throw against the wall.

Like a momentary touch
of fever, morning
dabs the top of the windowpane. I turn
to lie west toward the still clear
moon, a fullness
held in the fingers of a budding tree.
There is nothing to be done
by crying *moo, open,*
let me in, fill me, but I do.

Don't hurry, take time—
the story will begin again.

Chattanooga, 1983

The Disappearance: On Watching the USSR, August 21, 1991

When Mama's dark hair fell from its bun, her eyes wanting always
      wanting to convey
desire as she swayed gypsy-like—*O che chorniah*—she was traveling
      somewhere away from
in front of her eyes. One day I made her look at me: my first
      day of school.
She put a picture hat on her head to float me there. When

      she was dying
(her mouth an opening in a scream) she cried for *shav*, only
      the spinach borscht
from her Russian childhood—as if that milky soup would
      bring her mother
to take her where she had to go, as before to America,
      to the father
waiting on the dock, his long red beard, his dirty tie. Crowds
      pushing towards her—

pushing towards me this morning from the screen, Russian women,
      arms up, fists,
full bodies overturning all the words that in my childhood held
      enormous hope. The Revolution!
Arise! Join hands, *Freiheit*—it was the dream in our living room:
      out of sweatshops
men and women rallying, drinking tea night after night, saying soon
      happiness would come
to all if we unite. And that meant *life*—from my bed I heard it.
      And it disappeared
as if it never were worthwhile or real. How can life die?

The Inheritance

Just a grapefruit
but it never fails
to make the word *Mama*
when I cut it
store the half uneaten
flat against a plate
pink meat down
so that tomorrow
when I eat it it's as juicy
as today. Washing fruit
she taught us but never this.
She just did it. Saved
the fruit against the plate.
As I do. As I saw it done
in my daughter's house this morning.

Thrall to Iris

And I was wrestling that mystery, when, muscling free, memory
lifted off from
where it hides. Today is March the 21st, today is the day
my mother dies
and each year I put three iris in a vase to recognize her. If I forget her,
like a siren
she divides me. My head had banged like knocks on the door
all ordinary morning—
I'd let the heat of a shower enter my face, my shoulders, my hair,
but my eyes
wouldn't let up, throbbing, my nose kept clogged (with no tension
apparent to me).
As a vacuum sucks debris out of a rug, the apprehension of her death
clears my life
to hold her in it. My largest towel in her color, a Florida pink,
wraps her around
me to dry and dress myself the way you dress a doll and say
"errands to do"
and you take her out on them—to the flower shop where you request
from a man
the freshest ones which he goes into the refrigerated box to give you,
tightly tipped, purply-
blue, and, as iris do, they rise by evening; yellow throats
hidden in violet
now extend, pulling you towards their light, and always away
from their center.

Topless Dancer in a Dressing Room

(after a photograph by Diane Arbus)

All day she turns under sunlamps
to darken—except for breasts—
so when she's dressed
her breasts outshine
the feathered, sequined gown
designed to open on that whiteness.
Beautiful and calm
straight into the lens she stares:
> *Take me, come on*
> *take me—*

Her finger pushes
one white breast to make it shine out more.

I can't stop staring
at that frame, her breasts
so proud against the dark. My body
roars, bombarded by a drill: September
chilling leaves to new color, my daughter
off to Providence to begin her second year.
The door is closed on the flattened bed.
> I'm scared.

Sadness is turning into anger
turning breasts to fists. I want to break
from the clutter of a dressing room
and come out fighting.

I crack an egg
into warm, honeyed milk

and stir so there's no lump
stir until it's silk.
                    Come on, sweet cells, easy,
                    now don't gang up on me—
I pull the milk
through all my bones.
Still, I want a deeper sweet—
I lift the spoon, that sweet concave
from the honey jar, and lick it.

Three
———

In Greenwich Village on Halloween We Talk of Love

Dearest H., you'd have roared and carried on; hearty
laugher that you are, you would have clapped to see

such happiness. A high-heeled man in a silver sheath
threw chocolate kisses; a woman, wrapped paper leaf,

uncurled, became an undulating tongue of green snake—
and an old man who leaned as if to kiss my cheek
coughed golddust in my face. All night I sparkled.

But what I started to say, before the parade
got underway, had to do with love. The way

I love you. Waiting for the hoopla, I told my friend
I love you as the shore the wave. Set to marry

in December she wants to talk of love, what we
two do that's lasting. I said I love your going out
and I know you're coming back. As simple as that—

as putting on your robe—don't laugh—to be a nun
parading with a book, with women friends in sisterly

devotion, always knowing there's another, a man
(you) who gives me something else—less intensity?

touch, release. Fun—but weird to think of ordinary
love that way—right there on Bank where we once fought
about our first apartment—so scared we'd separate—

Just Now

Midnight, spring rain
and the city, expectant,
waits. I'm the Russian doll,

the one inside, intact.
My heart wants only to adore,   .
to stare from a window

seven stories high, above a door
held by a doorman at its side.
Buildings swell around me

rectangles of light.
Mercer Street's lamps bend
in a line towards the harbor
and on my corner an isolated man

bends under his umbrella.
I can't believe I've made it
to this innermost place: a cup,
a bed, four chairs around a table.

The House Warming

The father and mother crooned
over the perfect
        a pear
child, gentle as she grew
with little risings
        a berry
to a quiet beauty. An artist.
And then she died.

Some fearful thing is holed up
in this room
in this bare apartment
of a building built in 1931
        one year before my birth
        one year after my sister's death

where I insist on living—
But I don't resist
its presence—blue foil shining
in the dark, a brassy-something
angling toward my heart.

New York, Settling in the Sublet

"Sonia isn't in, no, she isn't in the city," I explain, "but I'd be glad to give your message." The quiet voice tells me Doris called. I spoon a soft-boiled egg into a cup, and the phone rings again. It's Doris whispering she isn't feeling good, asking how to take an enema. "Well, I don't, I mean I haven't . . ." I'm sputtering. Yet a woman is asking for my help. I summon reason: "Fill the bag halfway with water. Warm. Maybe you could buy one fixed, a Fleet"—reason's tricky—"oh, but you're afraid to go outside." I eat the egg. It's cold. Truck brakes grind five floors below. When the phone rings again Doris pleads, "If I come over, would you give me an enema?" I slam the phone and cry. And rig up a machine.

The Third Seduction: Talking to an Architect

It moves you
   over a threshold. He opens
   his book of rooms, bidding
you say *Yes*, say *No*,
   and as you do
   what hasn't mattered matters.
It comes across as love
   when someone wants to curve
   your ceiling and elevate
your bed. You skip a funeral,
   desire soffits, run after wood,
   stone, terra cotta tile—seduced
by the possibility
   of entertaining beauty,
   doors opening, you inside.

Art and Love

When I enter a museum and see
hundreds of potatoes, real
potatoes, earth grown,
stacked with bronze eyes of the artist,

and a man upon the ground, his penis
a tree growing straight up
to the frame, to leaves in the sky,
that tree, those potatoes

make me love nature. I buy high heels
to match a navy skirt and teal blouse,
sea colors I intend a change to—
flashier than volcanos.

Anointed I am an oily fish
radiant with passage—50 years
we fly to celebrate—to Greece, to Naufplia
beside the sea where, second night,

our room fills up with moon,
our seaside kitchen full of food.
He braids my hair with jasmine
trailing roots, I crown him

with a ring of seeded bread. Earth and sky
untie the sea: in every niche
the holy horniness of
Pan and the breasts of Aphrodite.

Shirley

I have had to wait this long to make a castle
out of sand, to let you amuse me,
to find each of my fingers kissed
for being there. It's a simple story—I was born
to a man and woman so besieged they could not love.
When I learned to read, then life began
in and through a book. Opening a mystery
I called out the name *Shirley*
penned on the flyleaf. My mother shrieked,
my father ran to me, closed the door, whispered
the story of their daughter dead at 11 in surgery.
They had never wanted another
he said. He was simply telling the story.
I was 11 when I opened her book. I couldn't die,
or it would kill my mother so I lived
carefully right—excelled in school,
married, gave birth. Then I was 45
and Mama died. She couldn't lose me anymore.
Only then did I write poetry, only for you
my dark brother, my nighttime dancer.

The Knowledge That I Have Everything in the Garden

for Fran

At 10:30 last night on 1st Avenue
a man in a black jacket
a tall man with a mustache
was picking out a cantaloupe.

O New York! You give me
63° and a whole moon
in November, pyramids of fruit
stacked up on the sidewalk

and my friend, I'm walking with
my arm around my friend,
coming from a play
that had 11 women talking with

a love for household lamps,
snakehandling, plastics
as an image of eternity, and, right here,
on your east side

a handsome man giving his nose
to the sweetness of a melon.

The Enormous Woman on the Uptown Bus

In the opening where the crowd thinned she
sprawled, legs apart, the enormous body
taking up a double seat and more, greasy

colorless hair limp beside the swollen face,
pink-lipstick mouth, her finger up her nose,
and I couldn't move. People filled the space

behind me, kept me there as if to show
me thighs (meaty, veined) she'd cocked so
I could see up to her v. I had to

push my way back into the middle of that bus
to lose her. I was terrified to see the chaos
of a door ajar that anyone, not just the light,

can enter! Here, in this city of my dreams,
what if I die? Having come to what I most desire—
saying that openly—what if someone robs me blind.

My mother kept her dreams locked in her heart.
She was a Beauty, though the guilt she suffered
after her child died—she once confessed

she'd made eyes at the surgeon—made her hide.
And the woman on the bus—all that flesh appeared
again not two weeks later, the flowered jersey

dress, the socks, the grey chenille-striped fur.
I wrote down what she looked like as if to snatch
some kind of victory, to make it matter that I look.

Eating Out

Risotto lovers of the world, we dine
on purple damask near the sky.

We who grew on stews
ladled straight from stove

to oilcloth always dreamed of elevating
skyward, and now, refined, we rise

to munch on slivered chives.
We tease our tongues with nuances:

sun dried tomatoes, raspberry coulis,
doodling in sauces and calling it

Versailles. Or so it feels, this
fussing over food to fancy it, or else

to criticize, to pick, to diet
as if by such denial to relish

emptiness—I'm so fat!—exercising
power over every morsel on a plate.

This Heart

for Harold

Yes I know I want what's real
so the seal stamped *solid brass*

fastened to the glass convinces
me to buy this picture frame

only a teenager would go for
or a lover with bad taste.

It's not easy being tacky, risking
a cliche to say I love you.

Poetry from such a place as
Have A Heart must be an urge

to have one, to say yes
to your polaroid and yes

to all the plastic of our clumsy lives,
yes to the hokum and the hooey

of a marriage neither young nor pure.
There's a porno thrill I get

in giving you this frame
in loving you with my eyes open.

Towers: Century City, LA

for Syud

Brazen flowers, they spring up, blocking the hills, casting
light from glass and steel,
like the limbs of men and women that pushed across a continent
to this expectant ocean. These towers
come from the guts of immigrants, from the chutzpah of moguls
for whom the stars in the sky
were not enough. They had to be defined, stood up to
with a platinum Jean Harlow.

On a crescent-curved balcony, 15 floors above
the Avenue of the Stars,
6 lanes of multi-colored metal traffic zipping back and forth,
in the middle a strip designed
not only to divide cars North and South but to entertain the traveler,
its eye of concrete,
grass and lily-shaped spigots projecting water skyward, cadenced kick

shush, shush, shush rocketting
over the rumble of motors, I am waiting for a birth, the birth of
our first grandchild,
the third generation conceived in this new world where—imagine it!—
the grandchild of a Rabbi
meets a Pakistani Muslim, they fall in love no matter what
we fear, and they will
have a baby whose name will be as old as

history. Benjamin.
And I will plant a garden with flowers for his eyes
because I will not be here,

because I want to give him a ground of many colors: coreopsis,
black-eyed Susans, my father's dahlias,
Mama's herbs—seeds that can be lifted by the wind or beaks
of birds flying over time-zones, oceans.

Last night I dreamed I watched for hours a baby's babbling
and twisting, babbling
and shifting, when suddenly he spoke—"Bon, bon" and then
"Good, good"—two languages!—
heavenly labials in a world of gutturals. In this city where angels
might fall at any moment,
I take as blessing the two-ness of his speech, believing
that such a start will save him.

From a Rock on Fishers Island

He's come here to fish. One stone, two stone,
three the one he stands on. Everything
round or flat, then the rise of
he's standing on a stone. That's all
I seem to want to say. He's come here
and placed himself on stones. To fish.
What I want to do is get to him. All I have,
thin line of rod angling from him.

He stands up in the ocean.
There is no tame ocean. Only here today
I keep dark things at bay, no, not me
but the day. It glides. It keeps me
out here with a stranger, with love of him.
New this love. Only that
I called my husband to give him my number
if he needed me. For the first time
I said: Call me, here is where I am.

What will come of such an ordinary thing?
Have I amputated longing? Have I given up
myself to a straight line
in the ocean? The ocean
is immense.
                    I break wind against the rock.
How pitiful I am in all this beauty! *Harumph,*
the old fart says, *quiet down.* Down and down.
Like the sun in the dune grass at my back.

He stands there fishing. The house stands on the hill.
The women in the house. And he can call.

Suddenly. Death a Flower

Before, I never saw death. Maybe
I was afraid of it and now, in daylight,
afraid of how easily I contained it
when it entered like a flower. Like a bread
simply rising on the table. As I slept
last night it rose between my breasts, an ache
blossoming, not sharp but round, zinnia
that would soon fill my mouth with its upwardness,
and like a terra cotta pot I was accepting it.

Accepting it, but I was alone, the house
alarm on, and if I had to dial
911 for help—that shrillness
going off like a mother, a father,
their dead child before me
whose funeral my mother wouldn't attend
filling every room, commotion
competing with and drowning out
my heart—I had to disengage it.

Dark. 4 a.m. 5. And I wouldn't be afraid
of someone breaking in in almost morning.
I was accepting it, the ache
branching, growing me out of myself
with the sinuous music of a synagogue service
crooking its melodies through my eyes
around the ground of my head with only my throat
having to close for the flower
that kept opening. I saw it.

Towers: Lower Broadway, NYC

Skyscrapers and canyons out beyond each window
are the mountains here. In the cleavage of these giants
we build home. My husband's left his place of birth

to stay with me, coming north with Tennessee
in tow—that's New York!—everyone arriving—*here I am*—
harboring visions, food, jokes. My father—I see him

in the cabinetry, bird's-eye maple worked by hand
along the bedroom wall drawing light from eight foot windows
which years ago enclosed a factory. Somewhere near,

women had to jump—all exits bolted tight—
I feel my mother's longing in these windows; it catches me
the way a mirror will when you pass yourself

and wonder who you are. Who is this
at 59, running after beauty, acting like a mother
needing desperately to be the one most

beautiful? We all desire more than to survive, not only
milk but spice and honey. I love this city, ferocious
heart charging my body, and I am here

to pitch my roof against its spires: Met Life pulsing
every hour (when your mother dies you know who's next)
and Chrysler, icy tree, rising on the Avenue,

offering me the sky broader than I ever saw
in Tennessee, changing every second, alive with
personality grand enough to stand beside the moon.

About the Author

Myra Shapiro, born in the Bronx, returned to New York after forty-five years in Georgia and Tennessee where she married, raised two daughters and worked as a librarian and teacher of English. Her poems have appeared in *Harvard Review*, *The Ohio Review* and other journals, and in many anthologies. She was awarded the New School's Dylan Thomas Poetry Award and is the recipient of two fellowships from The MacDowell Colony. She serves on the Board of Directors of Poets House, a library and meeting place for poets. This is her first full-length book.

Designed by Tree Swenson
in Palatino type.
Cover by Reginald Marsh,
Subway—14th Street (1930)
Hunter Museum of American Art,
Chattanooga, Tennessee.
Author photo by Lynn Saville.
Printed in China.